REDEFINE
REIMAGINE
RECREATE

The Proven Roadmap to Accelerate Your Business for Unprecedented Results

GW00468148

Andrew Satterley

First published by Ultimate World Publishing 2022
Copyright © 2022 Andrew Satterley

ISBN

Paperback: 978-1-922828-18-7
Ebook: 978-1-922828-19-4

Andrew Satterley has asserted his rights under the Copyright, Designs and Patents Act 1988 to be identified as the author of this work. The information in this book is based on the author's experiences and opinions. The publisher specifically disclaims responsibility for any adverse consequences which may result from use of the information contained herein. Permission to use information has been sought by the author. Any breaches will be rectified in further editions of the book.

All rights reserved. No part of this publication may be reproduced, stored in or introduced into a retrieval system, or transmitted in any form, or by any means (electronic, mechanical, photocopying, recording or otherwise) without the prior written permission of the author. Any person who does any unauthorised act in relation to this publication may be liable to criminal prosecution and civil claims for damages. Enquiries should be made through the publisher.

Cover design: Ultimate World Publishing
Layout and typesetting: Ultimate World Publishing
Editor: James Salmon

Ultimate World Publishing
Diamond Creek,
Victoria Australia 3089
www.writeabook.com.au

Testimonials

Andrew Satterley is a great leader who empowers his people and inspires them to be better than they ever thought they could be. Thank you for your inspiration, friendship and above all, your trust in me.

Bob Mules – General Manager, Almac Pacific

Andrew Satterley has been a global force in leadership and management in the Materials Handling and Access Equipment Industries for the last four decades.

We were lucky enough to be there with Andrew at Crown Equipment in the early eighties when it all began. It was like watching a gifted junior in the under 12s, you just knew he was going to be a champion.

Andrew's natural intelligence is at the core of his success. But not many are able to articulate their vision with the calmness and confidence that Andrew has proven over and over again.

As Melissa experienced first hand, Andrew has a unique ability to empower individuals to be their best and in turn, enhance the performance of the team and ultimately the business. We are so proud to have watched Andrew conquer the global business world and we are delighted that this book will now give so many an insight in the workings of the very clever mind of Andrew Satterley.

Melissa & Cliff Chadwick – Chadwick Forklifts Pty Ltd

I have known Andrew for the last 18 years where he has provided my organisation with professional coaching, marketing and general business consulting. In my 25-year career in business, I can honestly and confidently say that Andrew has been, by far, the most inspirational, diligent and talented professional I have had the pleasure of working with and for.

Fiona Duncan – HR Director, JLG Industries

I have never hesitated to seek Andrew out for his guidance, experience and business insights. I am fortunate enough to have a number of highly experienced and knowledgeable mentors, but I count Andrew among the best of them. His combination of business acumen, strategic thinking and strong ethical principles, make him a uniquely powerful influencer.

Jason LeGuier – CEO, Hotline IT

Dedication

This is for all the amazing people that I have been privileged to call my colleagues.

Thank you for your support, friendship and guidance over many years.

Dedication

Contents

Introduction

Having a great product won't guarantee business success, nor does being in business for many years. The reality is that success is never guaranteed and in a market we have never before seen, relying on the past will only make you vulnerable for the future.

In the last fifteen years, businesses have had to face and survive the global financial crisis, the emergence of not just China, but many Asian nations across every existing product line and new ones as they emerge, and more recently a global pandemic and war in Europe.

While these are amazing times, they are not unique. History has demonstrated that businesses have faced similar, if not worse times and survived, and many have boomed during or post these events. At the same time, many recognised and once successful companies have disappeared forever.

The question is, what ensures long-term success and sustainability for a business? Is it the products they sell? Is it their marketing? What is the magic formula?

In *Redefine, Reimagine, Recreate* I will propose that there is no magic formula, but rather some sound business and leadership principles that successful companies do better than their competition.

It starts with the three most important stakeholders a business has – its customers, its people and its suppliers – and how two-way engagement sets the platform for improved performance and lasting success. Most companies will agree with the premise, but very few get it right. Your stakeholders can provide an insight into your performance, quality and future, and even offer ideas you may have never considered that can be the way forward for your company. Imagine the impact if, through engagement, your customers or staff provided the business with an idea or a new direction that could take the business to a new level.

Every business focuses on new revenue streams and new sales, and while new business is important, it's your existing customers that provide you the basis for sustainable growth. They should already know the quality of your product and have experience dealing with you, and yet, they are often overlooked in the desire for new business. Knowing the detail of how you are perceived as a business provides you with a way forward to either maintain and improve on that perception, or to put actions in place to turn a negative perception into an ongoing positive experience and build a long and prosperous association for you and those customers.

I am sure that, like me, you have lamented the cost of replacing staff that have left your business. The reality is that this is one of the largest costs to a business, and not just in terms of the dollar value, but also the loss of experience and intellectual property. Ongoing staff engagement and understanding their perceptions, frustrations and what motivates them to be a part of the company not only reduces staff turnover, but is a major reason businesses succeed.

Business planning and implementation creates the platform for change and renewed success, no matter how the business is performing currently. In this book, I will use an example of a good business that became great and how that business learnt to listen, became agile and delivered for its stakeholders, and therefore itself. The misconception is that business planning is only for struggling companies or for new ones seeking finance, but for me, if you are not planning your future, you will soon exist only in the past.

Over my career and especially since I left the corporate world to assist businesses across many different market segments, I have seen a common theme. The businesses that embrace planning for the future achieve their goals, while those that resist or do it only to throw it in a drawer not only struggle, but in several cases close their doors.

What frustrates me in those examples is that they had a great product, great people and the market was there for them, but by not investing the time and energy to prepare for a changing market or circumstances, they ultimately failed. Maybe it was the personality of the leader – very entrepreneurial, but lacking the skills needed to drive a business plan. I have my theories, which is why I also cover the key leadership skills needed to drive a business through planning and change, and to build a winning team around you. Business leaders are not meant to be experts on every facet of the business and if they try to be, it can be a recipe for disaster, which is why having the right team is so important.

Every business can redefine, reimagine, and recreate itself and it's not that difficult. In fact, all you need is the drive to want to be better and the focus to follow the steps to make it happen. When considering where your business is at and where it goes next, I ask you to think about how much you have invested in marketing, your people, your product etc. then consider the following:

- Where are you now?
- Where do you want to be?
- How will you get there?

This is the essence of business planning and on setting the path for the future, and you should be asking these questions as a matter of course. If you invest money in marketing, staff, systems and so on, surely, you should invest time in setting the path forward.

Chapter 1

The Importance of Now

There is no more important time than now to consider redefining, reimagining and recreating your business.

Whether you are the business owner, the business leader, a senior executive or a manager, your obligations are to grow the business, mitigate risk, protect and develop your staff and to build sustainability for the future.

Even the most successful businesses face risk. What will make them truly successful is their ability to mitigate that risk, plan for the future, remain agile and constantly look to improve their position as circumstances change.

The size of the business or its market position does not alleviate the risk; instead, it will almost always mean that the risks are just different.

I'm not sure any of us have had to operate in more uncertain times than we have endured in the last few years. Whether you go back to the global financial crisis of 2008, which most people didn't see coming until it was upon us, or whether it's been the pandemic of today, an event which has potentially changed the way business is conducted forever. Both have changed the business landscape and many famous companies and household brand names have not survived.

That said, the reality is that business has always operated with changing circumstances, whether that be market conditions, economic conditions, government policy, technology, or opposition activity.

Successful and sustainable businesses share common traits. They plan for growth, plan for change, identify potential risks, are customer and staff centric and look for continuous improvement in all aspects of how they operate. It is a key part of their everyday operations, and it doesn't stop because their business is doing well. In fact, in most cases, the effort steps up as they realise that their success is also fuelling their competition.

Success can create the greatest risk to businesses that are doing well. Complacency or satisfaction can become the culture and that can mean that by the time the business realises it is losing 'its edge' it can be too late. We operate in an environment where those two concepts are potentially the most dangerous that a business can face.

If I may use a sporting analogy, the great baseballer Babe Ruth once said:

'Yesterday's home runs don't win tomorrow's games.'

This premise is as pertinent today as it was back then. Your success now does not guarantee success in the future.

The one certainty is that change will happen, and every business must be prepared for that change and where possible, be ahead of the curve. You want to be able to create stability and growth, drive positive change, lessen the risks, and improve the overall position of the business that you are charged with managing.

That is not to say that change is a bad thing. In a lot of circumstances, change has enhanced business performance. The unprecedented advance in technology is the most obvious example.

Just imagine not having mobile phones, email or the internet today. Believe it or not, business would still go on as it did right up till these became the norm. The reality was that companies that embraced this technology first gained a huge advantage on their competition. These were conscious, planned decisions by companies looking at gaining an edge, but companies also had to deal with an instant change in the business environment.

Before mobile phones, customers would ring the office, leave a message and understand that it could be one or maybe two business days before you would get back to them. The reality now is that if you don't respond to a phone call within five minutes, you'll see a text on your phone.

That is just an example of the change in expectation in the market that permeates both business and our lives in general.

So, business communication and responsiveness improved and as more advances came in, such as email and the internet, smart businesses continued to gain an advantage through technology. It did, however, come at a cost, and I'm not talking about the financial one. The impact on staff at the time was significant as expectation of being on call and contactable increased. Employees no longer worked a 9-5 day and this added strain on them at work and at home.

Smart companies embraced the technology, while the smartest ones also planned for the risks that could come with change, such as the negative impacts of the technology.

Now is the time to ensure your business is planning for the future as we know change will continue to come. Now is the time to ensure that you are better positioned than you've ever been before. Any business that is not creating a plan for the future will potentially be a business of the past.

I took over leadership of the Australian and New Zealand business of a global equipment company in 2007 and although I had created and successfully rolled out business plans in previous roles, it is what we as a team were able to achieve that I will refer to throughout the book. We were the market leader but as we dug deep into the business, we quickly realised how vulnerable we were and how poorly we were actually performing.

We conducted our business as our competition did, and not because it was the best way but rather because that's the way it had always been done.

We knew we had to redefine, reimagine, and recreate the business if it was to be sustainable, the dominant market leader, the employer of choice and the partner of choice within the marketplace.

While we planned change, our competition planned life as it had always been. I cannot stress enough how important this is and it works both ways. Creating a plan for the future can enhance your competitive advantage, while conversely, not planning will leave you vulnerable if your competition is.

By the time our major competitors even realised the changes that we had introduced, we were already a good two years ahead of them in terms of business performance, customer satisfaction and staff satisfaction, and we had built a business that was agile and able to change as needed.

Because of the uncertain environment in which we operate today, being agile and able to change direction is almost a prerequisite for any business that wants to succeed or enhance their existing success.

There was a time, and not a good time, in which when one year came to an end and the new year started, you would go through a budget process, looking at the previous year's results, creating forecasts and creating a new budget which was handed to the business. In my early management career, that was called business planning and it could take months. How that budget was turned into results was left up to each area to figure out, and if the numbers were not achieved, your future was not guaranteed.

That won't fly anymore – not that I ever think it really did. The reality is that, rather than having the budget dictate the plan, every business should be going through the business planning process, and the projected outcomes of that plan should be the basis for the budget. In addition, comparing financial results with the budget provides an overview of performance but does not explain either the why, or what is happening that impacts future results. Every business wants and needs to control the outcomes and that is challenging at any time, and I think even more so if you are not setting the path for the future.

Effective business planning allows you to understand your current situation and the challenges that exist. It will also allow you to set the goals for the future and then plan the roadmap from where you are to where you want to be.

It doesn't mean there won't be surprises or challenges along the way that you had not foreseen. However, you will be better positioned to meet those surprises or challenges as they occur.

If you have gone through the planning process effectively and developed a robust plan, that plan itself will be a living document that can be changed or altered as circumstances require.

Your staff will have ownership of their part of the plan, and they will understand the long-term goals. Effective communication will only enhance this and everyone in the business will be heading in the agreed direction with purpose and clarity.

If you are not planning, then your business is vulnerable to even potentially minor and certainly to significant changes that happen within the business environment. These reactive businesses are at the highest risk.

The assumption should be made that if you're not planning for the future your competition probably is. I want to stress this, as I've worked with many businesses in recent years that are reluctant to want to go through the planning process.

In many cases, the reluctance is because they're doing well now. That, as I mentioned earlier, is the complacency and satisfaction that puts you at the greatest risk.

To the businesses that say they don't have the time or need to plan, I will always advise, there is no better investment of time and resource than into the future of your business.

From a personal perspective, I can say that going through the planning process taught me more about the business I was leading than I ever could have learned by any other method.

It gave me a greater insight into our customers, our staff, and the business environment in which we were operating.

It enabled my team and I to set our strategy and initiatives for the future, create objectives and actions that we would undertake to improve the business, the customer relationship, and the satisfaction of our staff, while at the same time helping us create a sustainable business that was more ready for change than it had been ever before.

Strategic business planning gives your business purpose, empowers your staff, and builds stronger relationships with your customers.

Whether you're coaching a sports team, cooking a meal, or running a business, it's difficult to accomplish anything successfully without having a plan that takes you from where you are to where you want to be.

Creating and implementing an effective strategic business plan is reliant on understanding, and being able to answer the following questions, which will be discussed through the book:

- Where are we now? (Current status of the business)
- Where do we want to be? (Future status of the business)
- How do we get there? (The roadmap)
- Is it achievable? (Can we get there?)
- Can we change direction? (Being agile should circumstances change)
- How do we monitor success? (Checks and balances)

Often leaders that are reluctant to go through the planning process are uncomfortable with what they might uncover or hear about their business. I want to be uncomfortable. I want to know how the business is perceived by the key stakeholders. I want to know what the challenges the business faces are, because it's that information that's going to allow me to build a better business for the future.

So, let's get ready to be uncomfortable as we go through the key elements of building a winning business plan to redefine your expectations, reimagine the possibilities and recreate a winning business that is sustainable for the future.

The Importance of Now:

- Because next month or next year may be too late
- Because your staff deserve it
- Because your customers expect it
- Because your business future matters
- Because your success matters
- Because change is happening now
- Because your competition probably is
- Because success will not just happen
- Because if you don't move forward, you are actually moving backwards

Chapter 2

Reimagine Engagement

The first key question that needs to be answered to build a successful strategic business plan and to redefine the future of your business is, where are we now?

This is a review and understanding of the status of the business as it stands today. This will include a review of business performance against budgets and targets, and while this has to be done, just as critical and often ignored is to understand how the business is perceived by its key stakeholders. Planning preparation should therefore start with engaging with the three most important stakeholders: your customers, your staff, and your suppliers (business partners).

Even if you are not in the planning phase and just want to give your business a 'health check', engaging with the customers, the staff and the suppliers will provide you with invaluable insight into true business performance and the perceptions that impact the future.

You will learn more from interacting with these three groups than you will ever learn from reading financial reports. The reality is you will get honest feedback about how your business is performing externally and internally, uncover areas of improvement previously not known, and get a snapshot of the culture of the business, which cannot be understated in its importance.

Engagement involves two-way communication and should be part of the everyday operations of any business. How well you engage with your stakeholders will say a lot about your company and its current and future performance.

The most effective method in engaging with your customers and suppliers, especially when seeking to establish how your business is perceived, is to commission a survey, and I believe you should execute this through a third-party provider. While you can use your own people to do the work, the results are often tainted or watered down. Customers are less likely to be truly candid if they know they are talking with a staff member, especially if it is someone they deal with regularly, such as the sales team.

Staff surveys can be conducted internally as long as they are anonymous, so the staff feel comfortable to be open and honest. Human resources are best equipped to do this work and if you don't have an H.R department, then again, you can use a third party provider.

I want to go back to 2007, when I was new to the main seat. As part of being employed in the role I was given a brief on the business and its performance. It painted a picture of a solid, if not spectacular business that was market leader in our industry. We supplied access equipment, mainly to the hire and rental industry, although we also had a solid base of retail customers.

Within the business globally we were unique in that we also had an aftermarket service business, we ran parts, provided technical support and had a manufacturing facility that built products unique to the local market.

It should be noted that in the grand scheme of the global business, we were a small country in terms of equipment sales and overall revenue and profit, although locally we were number one and seemingly performing to an acceptable level.

It didn't take long for me to see the reality of how fragile the business was. In my first week, I received over a dozen phone calls from frustrated customers with various complaints ranging from quality issues, after sales service, communication, invoicing, and parts supply and for every phone call I received, my branches were getting at least two. I had also met with a number of customers across three states and while I was welcomed, I was also left in no doubt as to how they felt about dealing with our company.

I knew at this point that I needed to gain a better understanding of the issues and so I started the ball rolling by commissioning a customer survey. This started while I was at the airport heading back to my office from one of these state visits. I wanted the top ten customers to be surveyed face-to-face and the balance via the phone. In other words, no mass email surveys that would probably be ignored. For me, we had to show our customer base that we were serious about wanting to know how we were performing.

Satisfaction surveys are quite commonplace; however, I believe that most fail due to the way they are structured. Receiving an email or text request to 'rate our performance' is usually more annoying than effective and the response rate is poor.

Then you are asked to rate performance on a scale, which can be from one to ten as an example. I often wonder, if the common answer is a four or six, what does that tell the surveyor? How do they differentiate a six from a seven?

The other frustrating part of this type of survey is the lack of follow-up. I had an issue with one company's service, and they sent me this type of survey and I rated them at the bottom of their scale, and I added comments. That was two years ago and to date, I have heard nothing in return, which just further validates my reason for being annoyed with them and more importantly the ineffectiveness of this type of survey.

The aim is to engage with the group you are surveying, so from my point of view and to create effective feedback, the approach has to be more direct contact and pertinent questions that open discussion.

With this in mind, I created the questions, and while they covered a broad range of our performance and there was a dozen in total, the most important for me at the time were:

- What do we do well?
- What don't we do well?
- What are the most important areas of improvement needed?

I believed these three questions would give me the best insight into the issues that existed with dealing with our company.

The questions were direct and invited honest responses that potentially would be confronting, but that's what I and the business needed, and I would always advise this approach. Even the most successful and respected business will have areas that require improvement, and this type of survey will assist in uncovering the perceived issues.

You may not agree with the feedback you get, but if this is the perception, then it is the reality and should not be ignored.

When collating the feedback, you are looking for constant themes rather than a one-off issue. You will probably have an extreme or emotional response within the data; that one customer that has an axe to grind whose view isn't a true reflection of the overall business or responses.

While this should not be ignored and that customer contacted to work through the issue, your aim is to focus on the recurring themes or issues that the survey results present.

This is another benefit of having the survey conducted by a third party, as they will collate the data and present a summary of the uncovered issues, not the emotional responses. I had asked for a summary of the themes across all respondents, which I could then present to my management team. I did ask them to provide the raw responses also, but these were not used directly with my team.

Some customers named names and were quite personal with their responses and I didn't see any upside in showing this as my aim was to use the survey to build a plan for the future, a series of solutions, not to embarrass individuals or specific business functions.

The level of engagement was beyond my expectations. Nearly every customer contacted wanted to have their say. From this I knew we had issues, but I also realised we had a passionate customer base who wanted to work with us. That is a huge motivation to build a plan to improve the business.

The main outcomes included:

- Perceived as arrogant
- Poor communicators
- Lack of response to issues
- Equipment was great but issues existed with the paint
- Service was poor and long delays in fixing machines
- Parts supply was poor
- Inflexible
- Lack of product information
- Inconsistent
- Pricing

Most people reading this will think that pricing will always be raised as an issue, however I will counter that if all the other issues are resolved, then pricing is rarely an issue.

With this information, I set up a management meeting with three aims: firstly, to give a high-level overview of the survey results; secondly, to let the team know we would be embarking on building a strategic business plan; and finally, to start the discussion on what issues and challenges they felt the business was facing. This was important as it began dialogue on the key topics that we would detail at the business planning meeting and gave me the internal view of potential problems and opportunities as my team saw them.

I had a large group at this meeting. Every department and state was represented with the managers of those areas, as well as my direct management team.

There were varied reactions to the survey overview I presented, ranging from acceptance to outrage. The more we talked through the results, the more the team accepted and realised there was substance to the perceptions, and it wasn't personal.

How you present the findings is important as the information is usually confronting, and people's instinct is to take it personally. Summarise the key points rather than individual comments and just as importantly, reassure the team the results are the basis for improvement, not for retribution. This data, along with the staff and supplier's responses, will make the business planning easier and ensure we are focused on what matters and what will grow the future.

The staff survey was happening at the same time and the results would be ready by the time our strategic planning meeting was scheduled.

The staff survey followed a similar line of questioning as the customer survey as I wanted to know what the staff truly thought about the business, the tools they had to fulfill their roles, their future growth and aspirations, their frustrations and what they felt was needed to improve the business. Questions I asked included:

- What do you enjoy about your role?
- What, if anything, do you dislike about your role?
- What is needed to improve your area?
- Do you have the tools and systems need to complete your work?
- Where do you see yourself in the next five years?
- What areas should the business focus on to improve performance?

The engagement from the business, like the customers, exceeded my expectations and the feedback was for the most part a genuine attempt to raise real issues and concerns that impacted the staff's ability to do their role effectively. I think it is safe to generalise and say that people don't go to work to do a bad job, they don't want to see the business fail and they want to provide the best outcomes in each situation.

The results reflected this as the staff just wanted the systems, processes and tools to do their job well. They wanted training and opportunities for advancement, they wanted a voice, ongoing communication and they wanted to know the direction of the business.

They were clearly saying that this did not exist and when read in conjunction with the customer surveys, the correlation was obvious.

Their feedback became a large part of the business plan. If we were going to build sustainability, we had to ensure we addressed the issues our staff had raised. You will only be as good as the people you work with, you will only succeed if they succeed and you will only grow if they grow.

The third survey was of our suppliers and although it was a simpler survey the information received was just as important to the business. Without the support of and good working relationship with your suppliers you are potentially creating issues that impact your customers, staff and your overall performance. The focus was on what issues they faced having us as a customer and what we could do to make it easier to do business with us.

The results further confirmed the previous feedback. Poor systems, communication and being hard to deal with topped the list.

The next steps are key to better engagement. I wrote a letter to all our customers and suppliers, thanking them for taking the time to do the survey and summarising the results back to them, which demonstrated that we listened. I then outlined what actions we would be taking immediately and that we would be building a business plan based on the feedback that would be the basis for addressing the other concerns raised. It finished by asking for their patience and support as we undertook change.

While we provided regular updates, we were also conscious of not spamming our customers and therefore the updates were quarterly unless there was a milestone worth communicating.

The staff received an email with a similar structure although it had added focus on the journey ahead, their role and our need for their help. We then created a regular internal communication structure, which included updates from me via email, monthly branch barbeques and progress updates via their direct managers as a starting point.

If you report to a board, business partners or investors, then your engagement has to include them also. You want them to know how the business is perceived, but more importantly, you want to sow the seeds of the business plan and have their support in the journey. Once you have the feedback it is easier to gain support for the plan as long as you present the feedback with the next steps and potential outcomes.

You may not have all this as yet, but start the engagement and provide regular updates and seek approval for the next steps as you progress. Remember, this should be as important to them as it is to your business.

We began addressing the issues that we could prior to the strategic planning meeting as our actions were what mattered if we were to keep all groups engaged and there was plenty of positive change we could get started on immediately. This was not only good for morale but demonstrated to our staff, customers, and suppliers that we were serious about meeting their expectations.

Finally, prior to the strategic planning meeting we had to validate the feedback we had received and the issues that had been raised.

Every process and procedure we operated by was reviewed – all the systems, workflow and 'how we operated day to day'. This was exhaustive and not only validated the feedback, but also uncovered additional areas of concern that we needed to address.

It was clear that all the staff worked incredibly hard with poor tools, worse systems, little direction and while they strived to meet the customer demands, it was nigh on impossible with how they had to perform their duties.

While this may all seem daunting, it was actually exciting. Through effective engagement we had been able to do in three months what would have taken at least a year without the direction of our customers, staff, and suppliers. We had the foundation for change and at the same time we had the support of these key stakeholders, through effective communication, as well as time to achieve the desired outcomes.

No matter the size of your business or how long it has been operating, engaging with your customers, staff and suppliers will provide you with a true picture of your business. A picture of how it is perceived, its strengths and weaknesses and the opportunities that exist. Completed effectively, you will learn more about the true reality of your business and it will provide you with a basis for future business direction and purpose.

Reimagine Engagement:

- This is where planning the future commences
- Customers, staff, and suppliers
- Consistent, frequent two-way communication
- Their perception is the reality
- Direct contact, not mass emails or text
- Pertinent questions, rather than 'rate us' approach
- Summarise the feedback to the business
- Engagement is not a one-off
- Act on the feedback and keep everyone updated
- Engagement will enhance the customer relationship
- Engagement will empower and invigorate your people
- Effective engagement builds a better culture

Chapter 3

Recreate Preparation

As leaders we are always preparing, whether it is for a meeting, for a presentation, for the day ahead or any of the myriad of tasks that make up our day and our business. In essence, what is a business plan other than preparation for the future? The success of the strategic business planning process is in a large part dependant on preparation.

The time you spend with the team building the plan will vary based on the size of your business, however, even for a large company it should not take longer than three days on the assumption that you have prepared properly. The preparation doesn't end with the information gathered through the engagement and while you now have a basis for building your plan there is more to consider.

As part of the planning process, and prior to actually sitting down to create your plan, one of the key tasks should be to understand the needs and opportunities of the business.

Your engagement process will have uncovered or at least have you thinking about what is needed to meet the expectations of your customers, staff, and suppliers. The subsequent validation process will also highlight internal areas that have business needs if you are to meet those expectations. This could be anything from and is not limited to training, process and procedures, additional staff or even capital expenditure. Whatever this may be, it should be detailed as the business needs and become part of the overall strategic business plan.

The most obvious and essential need for our business was also going to be the most challenging. The business needed an operating system that could fulfill all the business functions and have seamless integration with our parent company system.

The business was using a 1960s green screen system that was so outdated and unsupported that it had fallen into 'death by spreadsheet' to keep functioning. Everything was paper-based and for the finance team, month-end would take two to three weeks to finalise. That meant the business could not make informed decisions or changes. By the time the managers had their results they could not address areas of concern as they were scrambling for the next month-end.

The aftermarket business was totally ineffective, but not because the team lacked motivation. They worked long hours with poor systems and tools and bore the brunt of customer frustration. Sticky notes were the main way to take customer call details and the controllers could not keep track of the technicians, the jobs, or the paperwork. The end result was an average of 1.1 jobs per day per technician (it should have been over three), many jobs not being invoiced, and a backlog that meant customers were waiting up to five days for someone to attend the problem. Add to this the lack of visibility and control of the parts business which meant parts went missing, slow moving parts or dead stock outweighed usable parts and therefore writing off six figure losses on parts was the standard.

This meant the work and preparation for a new system had to start prior to the actual strategic planning meeting. The business could not wait to formalise what we already knew. By the time we had our strategic planning meeting, we had already selected our systems provider and they presented the solution to the team during the meeting. This saved time, allowed the team to discuss the solution, not the need, provided the 'wow' factor and was invaluable in building morale and support.

If your engagement and validation also raise a need this critical, then I would suggest that you do not wait to be in the planning meeting to commence the project. In this case, I knew I would need approval from head office and supporting justification, however picking the system, having the supplier help build the justification and creating meaningful ROIs could be completed without committing to the system.

The more you prepare, the more easily the plan will come together and many of the objectives and actions will become self-evident. The plan will reflect the projects that have already started and that is acceptable. What is not acceptable is delaying critical projects that continue to harm the business performance and impact customers, staff, and suppliers as well as the bottom line.

It is not all about needs. Everything you have done so far will also uncover potential opportunities for the business that may not have been considered or known about prior.

As we went through engagement, we were made aware of the pending mining boom in our country and while we already knew the potential was there, we were told in detail about what was coming, and quickly saw the opportunity to invest in infrastructure in those regions and add additional mining specified machines to our factory orders.

We also realised there was a gap in finance solutions for the market and so set about finding a new finance partner that would offer the flexible solutions our customers needed. This partnership was so successful that eventually it was expanded globally, and they became the worldwide finance partner for the company.

Both of these opportunities became part of the plan and would play a significant part in the success that followed. I do not doubt that these and our other opportunities would have eventually been uncovered anyway, however, our planning process gave us the heads up early and allowed the business to properly plan and prepare. The end result was that our company was better positioned than our competition and we took full advantage in the years ahead.

If you are not planning, then you will miss opportunities or be reactive to them as you become aware. You will face additional challenges as you try to meet these opportunities as you may not have the resources, processes in place or the agility needed to take advantage of them.

Some of the opportunities we uncovered were more subtle in their impact. We added a customer care program to our list of opportunities as well as customer training. While we were clear that these would not result in an immediate betterment of the bottom line, we knew that both would improve the customer experience and loyalty, therefore providing a long-term benefit.

At this point we were just documenting the needs and opportunities, not fleshing them out. That came when the team was together building the plan. My other reason for just documenting the ideas was that I wanted the teams' input on what was put forward and I wanted to discuss in detail what they felt would and would not work and why.

Opportunities are not limited to external growth. You will also find internal opportunities that may be as simple as improving procedures for the business or developing the skills of the staff for their and the company's benefit.

The needs and opportunities had been taken from reviewing the survey data and the validation process. This does not mean everything had been captured and so having the management team submit their ideas or at least discuss what had been put forward was a crucial part of the strategic planning meeting.

It was also important that the plan was owned by everyone and if I created it and just presented it to the management team, it would be seen as my plan. For the plan to work, the team needed it to be their plan too. More than that, I also valued and needed their input.

Our customers had provided a lot of data around market conditions, such as the pending mining boom and planned infrastructure projects. This, combined with feedback from our suppliers and our own homework on economic changes and government policy changes, allowed us to detail and then factor in potential risks and further opportunities. All of this was essential in being prepared for building the plan.

The final part of the preparation was to have the team ready.

I sent out the agenda for the strategic planning meeting, which was scheduled to run over three days, and which included a planned team building exercise. The amount of time needed for something like this will vary depending on the size of your business, the number of attendees, and how effective your preparation has been.

All my team had been to head office, but few had visited other states and branches, therefore I planned the meeting to be held in one of those branches. I felt it was important for the team to see how the business looked and operated in other states. This also helped me during the meeting if I needed to emphasise certain points, such as the customer perception of inconsistent service across the business.

The content of the agenda sets the scene for what is to come and needs to establish the expectations and outcomes, therefore I believe it should start with the purpose and objectives of the meeting. It should also be structured as you want the plan to flow. As such, the agenda should start with the feedback headings from the engagement and preparation, which we detailed as:

- Customer expectations
- Staff expectations
- Business needs
- Business opportunities
- Market conditions

The agenda then followed the proposed business plan flow and included:

- Vision
- Competitive advantage
- Strategic initiatives
- Objectives
- Actions
- Accountability and timing
- Risk and mitigation
- Financial impacts

By the end of the meeting the strategic business plan should be agreed down to the business initiatives, objectives, actions, timelines, accountability and at least a basic understanding of the financial impact and return on investment the plan will deliver.

In addition to setting the agenda, I challenged the team to start thinking strategically and in terms of the outcomes. This included asking questions about where they saw the business now and where they saw it in the future. What did they think our competitive advantage was and what did they think the vision for the future should be?

At the time, I knew that not everyone understood the meaning of a competitive advantage and its importance, and I also knew that to most, a vision was seen as necessary but irrelevant. In other words, they thought every business puts out a vision, but only because it's expected. I needed to challenge this thinking as the vision was paramount to where the plan would take the business. So, from my perspective, these two questions of the team prior to the meeting were essential to them being prepared for what lay ahead.

I also wanted to challenge the thinking on what they thought they knew and how the business operated. As an example, the aftermarket business (service and parts) was never seen as a viable profit centre, but rather a necessary service provided to the customers. Experience suggested that the aftermarket business should be one of the most profitable business units and was critical to customer satisfaction and in turn future machine sales.

Therefore, the next question I asked the team to consider was, what will you do if machines sales stopped and where would the revenue come from to ensure our survival? The aim of this was to have them thinking about the growth of aftermarket or new revenue streams not yet considered. Although we did not know it at the time, this became even more relevant as the global financial crisis was about to bite.

Machine sales would slow in the coming months, yet we ended up being in a strong position to meet that challenge and subsequently capitalise as the market rebounded. It was not a coincidence that the better we prepared and planned, the better the outcomes were.

Whatever your questions are, they need to be linked to what you now know from the information gathered and be pertinent to solving the issues, creating and maximising the opportunities, and challenging the team to reconsider what they think they know and to start to think outside the box.

At this time, I asked the finance team to build a forecast for the next two years on the basis of 'business as usual' but to add a column titled 'business plan impact'. This would be used during the planning meeting to validate the impact of the plan's proposed outcomes. The plan had to make sense financially and knowing the impact as we built the plan, not weeks later, was not only going to save time but just as importantly confirm we were on the right path.

To this point there should be little impact on staff productivity. In fact the preparation to now should have everyone engaged and looking forward to what is to come. This, however, relies on how well you have communicated the process, the reasons and what positive change is coming. It is amazing how energised a business will become when it has a voice and sees a better future, which is yet another reason why business planning is so important to the sustainability of any business.

Now this is the part where I could detail all the famous quotes about preparation, however I think we all know why preparation is essential to any business and any task within it. What I will say is, the preparation discussed to this point will save time, provide direction, engage the business, and lay the foundation for the strategic business plan and its outcomes.

Recreate Preparation to:

- Ready the business and your team
- Set the foundation for what is to come
- Uncover needs, opportunities, and market conditions
- Challenge the thinking
- Save time and create focus on what matters
- Create the vision for the future
- Layout the business plan format
- Create excitement and expectation

Chapter 4

Redefine the Future

You may call it a strategic plan, a business plan, or just the plan, but the name is not as important as its content and what it delivers. I have worked with businesses that didn't believe a strategic business plan was appropriate for them, as they 'weren't big enough' for one. So, I suggested we scrap the idea and build a business plan instead, which they jumped at. In the end the only difference was the name, but it mattered to their perception and therefore the engagement and end product.

The point is, don't get hung up on names. We live in a world of buzz words, but all that really matters is the concept of planning for your business and establishing the future path for your success, or at the very least, ensuring the existing path is achieving the desired outcomes.

Remember, developing a plan enables your business to create a roadmap from where you are today (the first key question) to where you want to be in the future (the second key question), while enabling the business to remain agile, and potentially avoid or at least navigate unforeseen changes that may occur in the future.

Where you want to be in the future starts with the vision and ends with a series of strategic initiatives, objectives and actions that are designed to fulfill that vision. Importantly, the plan will help create and deliver your competitive advantage.

An effective plan allows your business to provide clear direction to your customers and staff, create expected outcomes, prepare for changing circumstances and, when communicated properly, ensure all employees not only share the end goals, but know the role in the journey for themselves and the business.

Businesses that do not have a business plan are susceptible to even the most minor changes in market conditions, economic fluctuations, opposition activity and often have high staff turnover rates as staff are more likely to feel disengaged from the business. It is also important to remember that a budget is not a plan. In fact, the budget should be an outcome of the plan. That is not to diminish the importance of the budget, as it is a key part of ensuring the plan will deliver improved financial results and that the objectives and actions within the plan are financially viable.

Many businesses will choose to develop a five-year plan, although my preference would be a two-year plan and the reasons for that are simple. A five-year plan, by design, makes it hard to maintain and achieve the goals over such a long period. Key objectives and actions get lost or lose their significance as they might not be scheduled to commence for years to come.

It is harder to keep the business engaged over such a long period and circumstances will change a lot in that time frame, as will customer and staff feedback, so the plan can be outdated very quickly.

Two-year plans tend to be more dynamic, more in touch with the now and deliver results relevant to what is happening during the timeframe.

There is a place for a five-year plan, and it will depend on its purpose and the nature of your business. Either way, an annual review of the plan and the data used to create it should be a standard part of your calendar.

The ideal starting point of the planning meeting is to establish the future direction and the business purpose, and this is achieved by answering two fundamental questions:

- What is the vision (goal) for the future?
- What is our competitive advantage?

Vision is a much maligned and misused term. Most companies publish a vision statement but only a few seem to get it right. What started off as establishing the future goals of the business, has, over the years, become a public relations exercise with little connection to what it should be and why it should exist.

If you currently use a vision statement, can you articulate it? Do your staff know it and its meaning? And how does it relate to how your business operates day-to-day and for the future? If the answers to these questions are 'no', or 'I don't know', then your vision is ineffective, and your business has not clearly stated its future goals.

The vision should be what your business would like to become, achieve, or accomplish in the mid to long-term. It should serve as a clear guide for defining your path. It's that simple, and it sets the foundation for the planning and for the direction.

The vision is where you want to be and is the agreed, future path of the business.

An effective vision will:

- Give the business purpose
- Motivate, energise, and align management and staff
- Be the foundation for decision-making
- Provide the basis for the business plan
- Provide clarity on business objectives

I am sure we all understand why vision statements are written the way they are today, however I would always advise to keep it simple and meaningful in terms of what it is you want the business to become and ensure the reader understands your future path.

Coca-Cola is my favourite example of effective vision. While their vision has changed over the years as part of their growth, one of their original vision statements was:

'Ensure that wherever you are in the world,
you can buy a coke'.

That simple future goal drove their strategy, objectives and actions and led to unprecedented market dominance at that time. For anyone who has travelled, I am sure you would agree that no matter where you are and how remote you may be, you can find somewhere to buy a coke.

It gave their sales and marketing teams purpose and direction, it led to innovative thinking such as vending machines for areas where a corner store didn't exist and gave them their competitive advantage that meant their competition spent decades just trying to catch up.

You don't have to use the term vision. Smaller businesses often just call it their goal and I have seen terms such as 'our future', 'purpose' and 'aspiration'. It's what it means to your business, staff, and customers that matters.

When we started our meeting, I proposed a vision built from the engagement feedback, the opportunities we had uncovered and where I wanted the business to be. Our parent company already had a vision statement, however we had a unique business model within the global organisation and it just didn't relate to our business or the future goals for our market. We didn't abandon the global vision – in fact we published both – it was just our vision that drove our plan and our activities.

As part of their preparation, I had already asked the team where they saw the future and what their vision of that future might be. In addition, they had the engagement feedback and we reviewed how the business was perceived and incorporated the expectations of our stakeholders into what our vision should be.

The vision had to meet those expectations to ensure the plan and the future aligned with our customers, staff, and suppliers. This meant this part of the meeting flowed well and by using my vision as a starting point, we quickly established our future vision for the business and were able to create a picture of where we wanted to be.

The plan now had a vision which incorporated several goals.

I would always suggest and recommend that the goals or vision are published and that all your staff are aware of what those goals or visions are for the future and why it is the vision. You want and need everybody aligned, to maintain the momentum, and keep the engagement you have started as it is one of the keys to long-term success.

The second fundamental question we addressed at the beginning of our planning meeting was to understand or create our competitive advantage. The plan was to be built to deliver and enhance the competitive advantage, so understanding it at the beginning is essential.

Your competitive advantage is what you do, or offer, that your competition cannot match, and every business should be striving to create or enhance their competitive advantage.

The competitive advantage will put your business in a more favourable or superior position to your competition because by definition, they cannot match you, and it is the basis for building long-term sustainability.

Jack Welch, the former chairman and CEO of General Electric said it best:

> *'If you don't have a competitive advantage,*
> *don't compete'.*

If you don't have a competitive advantage, you will be competing on price and your margins and sales will suffer, especially if your competition offers something unique. Every business needs to differentiate themselves from their competition if they are to survive and if it's based on price, then it is having a long-term impact on profitability and sustainability.

The reality is that price may give you a short-term gain, but it's hard to regain margin once discounted prices become the standard.

The forklift industry is a prime example. Equipment now is cheaper than it was 25 years ago, yet the quality, features and reliability are better than they have ever been. As competition has increased, especially from Asia, the pressure on pricing has meant lower margins and the need for the forklift companies to find something new to keep themselves ahead of the pack.

Even if pricing has been retained, it relates poorly to the cost of the build, wages and infrastructure needed and therefore the margins remain low.

Finding something unique that your competition does not offer is more beneficial, more sustainable and can in fact have a positive impact on your price position.

As we commenced our strategic planning meeting, most of the team had never considered the competitive advantage, what it was, what it meant and why it mattered. By the time we finished, however, it was established, it was meaningful, and it was at the heart of the plan we built and the success that followed.

For us, it already existed and was made obvious from the customer engagement. In simple terms, it was that we were the only company that offered a complete company-owned aftermarket business to support our sales and our customers. Up until this point though, it had not been focused on and was seen internally as a cost of doing business, not the basis for growth. Yet it impacted our performance in every aspect of our business. Poor service meant reduced sales and a dissatisfied customer base. It was a large part of the negative perceptions of our business and yet, presented our greatest opportunity. If we got it right, we knew it would be our competitive advantage.

By knowing this, we were able to focus much of the plan on resourcing the aftermarket business, installing the systems and processes needed and addressing the concerns raised by our customers.

Our marketing approach changed from selling equipment to being a better partner and we focused on gaining or regaining the service work of our customers. Our response time went from days to an average of two hours, and we started to win back our customer base.

Our technicians went from averaging 1.1 jobs per day to 3.8. So, while the cost of a technician hadn't changed, their return had more than tripled. Most importantly, we were meeting the needs of our customers, which in turn meant that they invested more in our business. The aftermarket business became a critical profit centre and as a consequence, sales increased dramatically. Our staff now had the tools to do their jobs and as such, their satisfaction levels rose, as did the overall morale.

We had found and built our competitive advantage, which our competition could not match. At the same time, we had improved our customer service, supported the needs of our staff, increased machine sales and turned the aftermarket business into a key profit centre.

If you are not aware of your competitive advantage or don't believe it yet exists, then time spent developing it will be a key part of building the plan and usually the opportunity will be somewhere in the feedback you have received or in understanding what your market wants and needs.

Even if you have a successful competitive advantage and don't think you need to be planning, then consider this – a competitive advantage has a lifespan. Eventually, and especially if you have had success, your competition will mimic what you have done and will not only copy your success, but also will try to add something unique to create their competitive edge.

We were now armed with all the information from the engagement and preparation process and had established a clear vision (goal) for the future while understanding and focusing on our competitive advantage. This meant that we were now able to build the business plan initiatives, objectives, and actions to achieve the vision and take advantage of our competitive advantage while meeting the needs and expectations of our customers, staff, and suppliers.

The importance of a logical flow to the planning process and keeping the team focused and engaged cannot be understated. Gaining acceptance and ensuring they understand and agree with each part is pivotal when it comes time for them to communicate with their teams and for the successful implementation of the plan.

The team could see how all the parts were connecting and their significance. It was the next part, however, that would determine how effective the plan would be.

This is about redefining the business they think they know and having them accept and support change through their part of the business.

Redefine the Future:

- Create and understand the vision (goal)
- Own the vision, share the vision
- Establish and build your competitive advantage
- Link the engagement feedback
- Ensure they align
- Challenge what the team think they know
- Logical flow creates understanding
- Communication
- Continue building excitement and expectation

Chapter 5

Reimagine the Plan

Building the plan with your team should be exciting, full of passion, robust discussion, exchanging of ideas, and fun. You are building a roadmap for the future and that should have yourself and your team pumped.

You have established 'where you are' from the feedback and business reviews, through the vision 'where you want to be', and now you will map out 'how we get there', which is the plan.

There are many ways to structure the plan and the preferred layout is not as important as the content. The plan must create the activities that will address the feedback from the stakeholder engagement, meet the business needs and take advantage of the opportunities that have been uncovered. As you build your plan, you should be checking it against the vision for the future and your competitive advantage, to ensure it delivers both.

My preferred structure is a plan that is made up of a series of objectives and actions created to achieve the strategic initiatives. Strategic initiatives are the overarching means by which you translate the vision (goals) into performance changes.

In most cases you would have four or maybe five strategic initiatives. In our scenario, we had five. Our first initiative was to 'improve the customer experience'. If the preparation has been completed properly, the feedback from your stakeholders and the data collated around business needs and opportunities will make establishing the initiatives relatively easy.

I bullet pointed all this data during the planning meeting and as we reviewed it, we were able to summarise the information to headings and these headings became our initiatives.

Each initiative, its objectives and actions were focused on improving areas of concern, addressing business needs, meeting the expectations of customers, staff, and suppliers, achieving the vision, and establishing the competitive advantage, all while improving the overall financial performance of the business. In other words, none of this is random or happens by accident. This is a process to build a better business, no matter how successful you have been to this point.

Once the initiatives are established it is time to create the objectives and the actions needed to achieve them. You should have all the information you need to make this happen.

If the initiatives are the overarching means to achieving the vision (goals), then the objectives are the specific goals needed to make it happen. How many objectives you create will depend on the initiative and on the information you are using to build your plan.

Our number of objectives varied from just one up to ten. Where possible, the objectives should have targets attached, targets which need to be realistic while also demonstrating the improvement in performance expected.

For our initiative of 'improving the customer experience', we created six objectives, the first of which was to 'improve service response times, with a target of two hours'. You may remember, I mentioned that our response time had been measured in days, not hours, something which was a major concern to our customers and had led to a loss of business (both sales and service) and had a significant impact on our financial performance.

We took the time to discuss the impact of achieving the objectives we set. This is important for several reasons. The objectives must be achievable, must be financially viable and must deliver the desired outcome (the strategic initiative), which in this case was to improve the customer experience.

This objective had four specific actions created, but again, the number of actions required will depend on the objective and the scope of work needed. The actions are specific work the business will undertake to achieve the objective. The actions are where much of the discussion tends to happen.

The actions must be realistic and achievable. It would be unrealistic for us to have proposed adding another fifty technicians as the action to improve response times. The problem wasn't the number of technicians, but rather the way in which we operated and our efficiencies. In addition, the financial modelling would never have stacked up.

For all the actions proposed I had the finance team do real time modelling (during the planning meeting) of the cost and the return on that cost. This enabled relatively quick analysis and was an invaluable help in building a realistic plan.

The return on investment is not always obvious. If you need to add additional staff that are not revenue generating, for example, then it may initially look like a cost without return. When you analyse it further, however, the return may come from improved internal performance, which in turn impacts the customer experience or may take the stress off another department or other staff. This can improve productivity and therefore does have a financial return.

The actions are where most of the planning time is spent and if you have a large team in the meeting, you will have a lot of actions proposed and needing review. This is a good outcome though, as it is where the engagement peaks and the team begins to truly own the plan.

If you lead a small business or have a small team and you are putting the bulk of the plan together, especially the objectives and actions, then I would always recommend you engage someone outside the business to discuss and possibly challenge each objective and action. At the very least you could have your accountant check the financial impact of each action to ensure your plan's viability.

Working through the example I have been using, the initiative was to 'improve the customer experience', one of the six objectives was to 'improve service response time with a target of two hours', and one of the four actions was the 'stock service vans with relevant parts'.

Our preparation had uncovered that our technicians were losing up to 30% of their time returning to collect or waiting for parts to be delivered to them on-site. We further established that there was little or no structure to the parts they carried, and it didn't relate to much of the work they were allocated. In short, we had no parts management system for the service vans.

A key part of the plan we were building was a new operating system, which included state of the art in-van terminals and automated parts management, and this was a capital investment that the plan relied on and was covered across several actions and objectives and all the strategic initiatives. That did not mean we could not start this action and improve the way we managed parts within the vans and, if we didn't get approval for the system, we would have to anyway.

We established that we could, even without a new system, reduce the 30% lost time waiting for parts to 15%. That meant our technicians could complete one additional job per day and our service response time would improve by 20%, which meant the action was essential to meet the objective and the initiative.

Not every action will deliver the perfect outcome initially, however if the actions trend you to the objective and can be improved upon over time, then they remain valid. As it happens, we did get approval for the new system and we subsequently hit every objective, but the system took fifteen months from approval to go live. Despite this, we were able to deliver improvements to our customers within weeks by simply focusing on the action we created.

Now the plan is taking shape. You have the strategic initiatives and you have created the objectives and actions needed to hit those objectives. All the preparation data should be ticked off as addressed by the objectives and actions. The next step is to allocate timelines and people to the actions.

Every action must be time critical, and I believe it should be by agreeing a start date. Some plans I have seen use an end date, however I think this then slows your progress and can lead to failure as people wait till the last minute to get started and you don't have the initial sense of urgency needed. It is also harder to monitor where the plan is at, and it makes review meetings and updates to stakeholders look unprofessional if the key actions haven't yet started.

Allocating a lead to each action is just as important as the action itself. This person is the one who is committing to overseeing the action, allocating resources to it, reporting on progress and any issues that may arise and delivering the outcome.

In most instances, the lead is fairly obvious. For example, the national parts manager was allocated the action of 'stocking the service vans with the relevant parts'. If the action cuts across several areas, then you can either make the call or ask for a volunteer. I was very conscious of ensuring there was an even spread of the workload and even though it was not the lead's job to do all the work, it was their job to ensure the work was completed and remember, on top of their existing duties.

As the business leader I took on several lead roles, especially around the new operating system and some sales and marketing activities, as this was my area of expertise. What is important is that you are just as invested in the plan's objectives and actions as you expect your team to be.

The finance team completed the financial projections on the basis of achieving all the objectives. These financials included every detail, such as additional overheads, staff and the capex needed, while also showing the new revenue projections with timing linked to when the changes would occur.

Creating the financial modelling has additional benefits to validating the plan. If, like us, you need approval from head office, then having a detailed financial plan that reflected the business plan outcomes is essential. You may have a business that needs to gain financial support from investors or financial institutions to expand, buy new equipment etc. and the financial portion of the plan will be a necessary requirement for any of these groups.

The plan we built had five strategic initiatives, twenty-five objectives, and ninety-two actions. The timing on the action start dates was across an eight-month period and everyone in my team was a lead at least once. At this point, we had to address another of the strategic planning questions: 'Is it achievable?'

Once the planning meeting has finished the business plan document can be created and this is the right time to bring the team back together and ask, 'Is it achievable?' The business plan is now in a structured, easy-to-read format and going back through it and having a second look at the objectives and actions will allow you and your team to verify what has been previously agreed upon, and make any potential changes needed. It is ok to make changes and if any part of the plan appears unrealistic, then establish why and what needs to be done.

It is better to make changes rather than try to proceed with a plan or part of a plan that cannot be achieved. It is rare that the complete plan is not achievable, however it is common to make some changes once you have had more time to consider its content.

Building a risk and mitigation portion of the plan can also alleviate some of the concerns around achieving the plan's proposed outcomes.

We took this path and for each objective, we documented what the risk could be to achieving it, what the impact on the business would be if the risk was not addressed and what mitigation we would take to overcome the risk. This provided two benefits: firstly, we had a plan B and secondly, this part of the plan helped gain approval to proceed from head office as they could readily see the impact of not fulfilling the objectives, especially as we detailed the impact in dollar performance.

While ninety-two actions may seem a lot, many of the actions were able to be completed in a short period of time and improvements delivered externally and internally almost immediately.

This allowed the business to communicate positive change that was noticed by our customers and staff. In turn, this enhanced the engagement and our customers, due to the positive change, were more forgiving on areas that had not yet improved.

The plan made sense and was a direct reflection of what the business needed to do to meet the expectations of the stakeholders, fulfill the business needs and take advantage of the opportunities that were present. It gave the business a clear path from where it was to where it wanted to be, while building a competitive advantage.

The reality was the business embraced the challenge and was motivated by the possibilities of what the plan could deliver, and the culture began to change for the better. This was a key outcome as I was about to ask a large part of the business to take on extra responsibilities to execute the plan, especially as we went through implementing a new operating system.

The Importance of Now:

- Four or five strategic initiatives
- Objectives are the specific goals
- Actions are the work needed to achieve the objectives
- Timelines and leads
- Financial impact of the plan
- This is the roadmap
- Is it achievable?
- Risk and mitigation

Chapter 6

Recreate Implementation

The implementation process is as critical as the plan itself to the overall success of the business. Poor implementation may mean the planned outcomes are delayed or not achieved at all, and can also mean disengaging your staff and the customer base.

Conversely, structured and disciplined implementation may see the results exceed expectation or be achieved earlier than planned, while reinvigorating your staff and the customer base.

There are eight fundamental principles of effective implementation:

- Approval
- Commitment
- Communication
- Accountability
- Review
- Agility
- Change management
- Monitoring success

Depending on the business and its structure, you may need to have the business plan approved, either by a head office, investors, a board, or business partners. This especially applies if your plan includes additional resources, such as headcount, capital expenditure or any form of spending that is outside budget guidelines.

Our plan was a prime example. The business plan had additional headcount, an operating system and facility upgrades, as a start. We were asking for several million dollars and while we believed the plan had ample justification and built-in return on investment, we had to overcome two challenges. The first was that the company had put a freeze on all headcount and capital expenditure as the global financial crisis had started to impact the business globally. The second challenge was one that was always going to occur, which was having head office believe in our plan and our vision for the future.

While we had built a risk and mitigation plan which would allow much of the plan to proceed without the requested funds, the reality was that the significant improvements were dependent on these funds. I also had to consider that my team and our business were so invested in what the plan meant, that to not get approval would simply be a disaster.

I had to go to America for another meeting and I had the plan under my arm and had requested to spend time with the president of the company to detail the plan.

I was given a 20-minute meeting, which was never going to be enough time to go through the plan in all its detail. So, I gave a high-level presentation that focused on where we were, where we wanted to be and how we would get there and finished by giving an overview of what we would deliver back.

With the American and European businesses reeling from the financial crisis, the company needed to find an area of growth and I committed that if the plan was approved, we would be that region. I left the meeting without an answer.

No sooner had I landed back in Australia than there was a message from the president to say that he had reviewed the plan and that he and a couple of the senior vice presidents were coming to Australia.

They wanted to see for themselves where we were and where we wanted to get to. I was nervously excited, but welcomed the opportunity, as I firmly believed in what we were trying to do and the plan we had built.

When they arrived in Australia, we took them around our branches, especially the ones we wanted to spend money on upgrading. There were meetings set up with our key customers, with the focus on hearing again the feedback from the surveys. We gave a demonstration on the new operating system that we wanted to roll out and a complete, detailed overview of all the actions and potential outcomes that we had put into our plan. We had also taken the opportunity to create business case documents for each capex item requested and we were aggressive and confident in the return on investments within those documents.

They quickly grasped our vision and the potential that the plan provided, and we gained the approval to proceed, while being reminded that failure was not an option. I was genuinely excited to take that pressure as I believed in the plan, how we had created it and what it would deliver.

I also knew America believed in our plan as we were the only region to be given capex and funds for additional staff, and it was no coincidence that we were also the only region to submit a strategic business plan.

If you do need to gain approval for your plan, then trust in the plan and what it will deliver.

That belief is the essence of commitment. As the business leader it starts and ends with you as you cannot expect the business to be committed to the implementation of the plan if you are not. You will be asking staff to take on additional responsibilities as you complete the objectives and actions, and you must lead from the front.

Commitment flows through every aspect of the implementation, from ongoing communication through to change management and all aspects in between. Depending on how much needs to be done to implement your plan, there can be times where the business feels overwhelmed, an aspect is not on time, or a problem has arisen, and it is when these things happen that your leadership matters.

At times you will need to be a mentor, a motivator, a peacemaker, a sympathetic shoulder, and the person who brings the implementation back in line. All of these are traits of a good leader and of commitment to a successful implementation.

Communication is what started the planning process and it is vital to every part of the journey towards building a better business. Effective communication creates momentum, excitement, and maintains focus for your business and for your stakeholders.

It also allows you to gain support should issues arise as your staff, customers and suppliers are more likely to be understanding if they are a part of the journey, know what you are trying to achieve and see the benefits that will come for them.

The messaging is really important to ensure that the staff are aware that the plan will bring change, growth and business improvements, but also that it is there to make their lives easier, to improve their job satisfaction, as well as to improve the business culture in which they operate. This cannot be understated. A business plan that doesn't improve the culture of a business is doomed for failure. Even if the change is only small, it should be an improvement for your staff, and as such, the staff are more likely to welcome that change.

Regular updates on the implementation, the results being achieved, and next steps is the simplest way to communicate and as always, I would suggest you invite two-way communication as this will enhance your position.

The business plan has a level of accountability built in as you have leads for each objective and action created, however, that is not enough. Providing a structure, guidelines, and a reporting process will give your team confidence in what they are doing and creates accountability.

I created a simple document that outlined the role of the lead, the expectations, and some simple steps on how to proceed. Your approach will depend on the size of your team and the number of objectives and actions within your plan, but the idea is to have a consistent approach and to set the expectations on how the implementation will proceed.

That leads into the review process. The review process that you adopt will enhance the accountability, allow the business to work through any issues that arise and keep everyone focused. So, getting the review process right is essential.

I held a weekly staff meeting each Monday morning with a standard agenda and once the implementation commenced, the progress of the plan became the starting point for each meeting and all the leads were invited for that part of the meeting. We reviewed the status of each action that was underway and followed the guidelines that had been laid out in the document created for the leads, which included:

- Status versus initial timing
- Issues or challenges
- Outcomes and business impact
- Next steps
- Resources

When needed, I invited the relevant suppliers to present their updates on progress. For the company developing the new operating system, that was nearly every week.

By having these weekly meetings, we were able to address issues quickly and create corrective action when required. It was important, from my perspective, to keep the meetings fast-paced and focused and everything was minuted, which gave the team a reference point once they left the room.

How you structure your review process will again depend on the size of your business and the plan you are implementing. What matters is being consistent, as this maintains focus and progress.

Question five in the planning process is, 'Can we change direction?' And the answer is yes.

I am often asked: how does a business plan keep you agile, as isn't it locking you into a set path forward? My reply is, if you have an effective implementation process that encompasses all the elements we have discussed in this chapter, then that creates agility. Every successful company I have known is agile and well-positioned to change should change be required.

Circumstances can and often do change while you are mid-plan, but if you have regular reviews, you will pick up on those changes quickly. This will allow you to potentially modify a particular objective, put it on hold, drop it altogether or replace it with a new one. The weekly meetings allowed us to perform a health check, not just on our progress, but on the ongoing relevance of each of the objectives and actions that we had created. There was no point in completing an objective that may no longer have been relevant or added benefit due to changes in the business environment.

We had built our marketing activities into our plan by creating specific marketing actions that would enhance the objectives. When the global financial crisis began to impact our market, we were able to modify our marketing to meet that change. Many of our customers put machine purchases on hold due to the uncertainty, so we quickly realised that these customers would rely more on older, existing equipment. We then changed our plan and began a new campaign designed to 'support you through tough times'. This was aimed at building our aftermarket business while assisting our customers to continue to meet their market needs. It was a huge success for our customers and for us, and it also showed that we were agile and able to change as circumstances dictated while still achieving the strategic aims of the plan. It had the added benefit of building a lasting loyalty between our company and our customers.

Changes, should they occur, will need to be factored into the financial modelling you have created. This will give you a clear understanding of the impact on the business. You can then communicate the change, the reasons why and set or modify the expectations without losing momentum or purpose.

One of the great challenges of any business is change management and not just when implementing a business plan. It is human nature to resist change and I lost count of how many times I heard 'but we have always done it this way'.

This is an opportunity rather than a problem, and being aware that change is not easy for a lot of people is the first step. Understanding that because some of your team may resist change does not devalue their importance is the second.

I have found through my career that the keys to successful change management are:

- Communication
- Engagement
- Inclusion in the change
- Benefits of the change

You may have noticed a theme around communication and engagement throughout the book and that is because these are two of your most powerful tools as a leader.

The expectation that change is coming has been established very early on through the engagement, feedback and the ongoing communication. The quality of the communication is what will keep people engaged. The communication should outline the current situation, the reason for change, what the changes are and importantly, how it will benefit them in their role and overall job satisfaction.

The communication style also matters. This is not a time to be dictating to the business – the communication should be inviting, and the theme should be that of seeking assistance rather than insistent. The reality, when implementing a business plan, is that you will need the team's help and their inclusion in developing the change is vital to the outcome.

Moving our service tecnicians to a paperless system was identified as the most significant change management challenge within our overall plan. There was a large part of that team that were 'technology adverse', and an even larger part that saw the changes as big brother looking over their shoulder.

We could have forced the changes and worn the consequences of potentially losing some of the team or creating an 'us and them' culture, or we could engage them, seek their help and have them help us create the new system. We chose the latter.

We started by setting up team meetings in each location. With this type of change, the communication needed to be face-to-face and interactive. We outlined the changes, the reasons, and the benefits to them and to the business. We asked for their feedback and discussed their concerns. We then asked for them to help us create the change and asked for volunteers to test the handheld devices and scanners that they would be using. This is and was a key element of change.

Having the team included disarmed a lot of the resistance as the technicians trusted their colleagues more than management. I should note that many of the volunteers were the most vocal critics initially and by their own admission wanted to see the changes fail, but we welcomed that scenario as winning their trust would only help the overall acceptance. It also made sense for the business as these were the people at the coal face and their input would enhance the end product.

The volunteers, over time, became champions of the changes and were our greatest asset in convincing the rest of the technicians that the changes were a good thing. They took on the role of training their colleagues, without being asked, and were an integral part of the successful roll-out of the system and the results that followed. They demonstrated and sold the benefits of the system for the technicians better than we ever could and without putting too fine a point on it, our adversaries became our allies, which created a culture of cooperation that lasted long after the plan was implemented.

We continued the direct communication throughout the implementation via monthly face-to-face meetings and continued to listen to and address concerns, challenges, and any other issues that arose. These meetings continued post-implementation and were a standard part of our operations moving forward.

Not all the changes that the business plan delivered were as challenging, however even when change was embraced, the principles of change management were still used.

The final question of building an effective strategic business plan is, 'How do we monitor success?' This comes in two parts: the first is during the implementation and the second is the ongoing monitoring, post-implementation.

Your review meetings are the forum for the checks and balances and setting the expectations on performance should be completed early in the implementation. You have allocated the leads to the actions and objectives and provided an outline on their roles, and as part of this you will establish the timelines on completing the tasks. The timelines then become the first metric of success.

Meeting timelines is vital as many of the actions will crossover each other and you do not want actions being on hold while waiting for others to be completed. Therefore, setting realistic timelines based on the requirements of each action is essential. Momentum and morale need to be maintained and unrealistic completion goals that cannot be met will impact both.

As actions are completed it is reasonable to expect seeing the objective targets being met or, at the very least, progress towards that. Depending on the objective, this might be done via improved revenue performance, cost reductions, improved productivity etc. By design, the plan will have outlined these performance expectations and these will become your success points for review. Success at this stage is not the same as the success you will expect once the plan is fully implemented.

Reviewing the impact on the business and the stakeholders during the implementation is also a good guide to the success of your progress. While you do not need to do a full engagement survey during this period, meeting with customers and staff and discussing your progress is a great way to monitor success and gain invaluable feedback as to the impact on them.

Once the plan is fully implemented your expectations on success will be very different and as part of creating the plan, you will have built in the financial expectations, as well as the targets established for each objective. Again, these are not always financial. We had several that involved staff retention, training and customer satisfaction as examples, but we still created expected outcomes that we could monitor our success against.

The objective targets against the strategic initiatives became the business metrics that we operated by and were used for business performance reviews.

Implementation requires focus, discipline, determination, hard work and constant communication. No matter the size of your business or the plan, in most cases, every staff member will have a role to play while also continuing their day-to-day duties. Therefore, how well you approach the implementation will not just impact the financial performance, but also the business culture.

Recreate Implementation:

- Gain approval
- Commitment to the implementation
- Effective communication
- Ensure accountability
- Review process
- Stay agile
- Change management
- Monitor success
- Build a better culture

Chapter 7

Reimagine Leadership

I am hoping, as you read through my book, that you realise how important your leadership is to the success of redefining your business. Every leader has their own style, and that style has got you to where you are today, so this chapter is not about teaching leadership or comparing leadership styles. There are, however, some important elements or traits of leadership that make a difference when creating and implementing a strategic business plan.

Your leadership matters. Whether you are creating and implementing a strategic business plan or navigating the day-to-day operations of the business, either way, you set the culture and the standards by which the business performs and is perceived. So, if the culture was bad, I would always question the leadership and conversely, if the business was performing well, the customers and staff were happy, then the leader must have created a good culture.

I have seen the best and worst of leadership through my career and I learned valuable lessons from the good and the bad. I tried to adopt the traits of the best while learning what not to do from the worst. I want to make this point as poor leadership permeates through the business and the damage in many cases is irreversible, especially when taking the business through change.

One of the additional benefits of taking the business through strategic planning and implementation is watching people step up. You will learn a lot about your team, and you will uncover leaders for the future you might not have known or who aren't currently in leadership roles.

Consider also that great leaders are not necessarily people above you in the business – they can be peers, or even have roles beneath yours. What stands out is the traits they demonstrate when it matters.

The traits of great leadership begin with leaders being confident but not egotistical. Having the courage to make tough decisions and back your own judgement is very important, as is not allowing it to become all about you. The best leaders that I've worked with spend more time talking about their team than they do about themselves. Their team's achievements, the business's achievements – not their achievements.

It's a 'we', not 'I' mentality. When things are going well, we achieved it, but if things aren't going well, the best leaders take it on themselves. Then it's an 'I own up to this,' or 'I take responsibility for this,' and it makes sense. As a strong leader, you have empowered your team to fulfill their roles and their potential. When something goes wrong, it must sit with you. This is all part of the culture you're creating. When the business or specific areas are going well, then it must be about the people that made it happen. Even though it might have been your idea, or your instructions, the result is a 'we' result.

This attitude and approach will flow through the business and is one of the core elements of a winning business culture.

When taking a business through the strategic planning journey, this way of thinking will impact and motivate all your staff and builds strong culture. You started the process by engaging your staff and listening to their views on the business and this may have uncovered information that doesn't sit well, but perception is reality, and this is the perfect time to put your ego aside and take on board their thoughts and use it as a basis to build a better version of the business you lead.

You still need to be decisive and ultimately you are accountable for the plan, its implementation, and the outcomes, but you cannot do it alone and having the support of the business is imperative to achieving the vision.

Therefore, using influence rather than authority is also a key strength and follows on from the confidence, not ego trait. The authority comes with the role anyway, so it doesn't need to be forced on the business, while the influence you bring is a key to keeping the business excited, motivated, and eager to be a part of the plan's success.

Bringing people on board with your decisions and having them take those decisions as their own is a skill in itself, and the very best leaders do it very well. The tone of your communication and ongoing engagement is your opportunity to bring the business with you on the journey and have your staff own the plan as their own, while maintaining momentum and purpose.

Leading through inclusion and a shared vision of the outcomes empowers your people. Remember that you will be asking your staff to take on extra duties while the plan is implemented and potentially changing the way they do their work, so this is not a time to be autocratic. It is rare that, as the leader, you are also an expert in every aspect of the business and as such you, and the business, need the experts' opinions, feedback, and skills to succeed.

We are all taught that actions speak louder than words, and as a leader guiding a business through strategic planning, this should be at the front of your mind in every aspect of the planning process. Communication is a constant theme in effectively creating and implementing your future plans and as such your words matter greatly.

Effective communication matters because it is where you paint the picture, build excitement, gather support, and gain assistance for what is happening and what is to come. It will also be used to provide updates, recognise achievement, and keep the momentum going. Eventually though, words can lose their impact if the actions don't support what is being said. Therefore, it is what you are doing that will ultimately influence the business and your actions will determine the level of enthusiasm, engagement, and the outcomes.

Ensuring you take the lead on some of the key objectives is a good starting point as you are leading by example, taking ownership, and being accountable back to the business in achieving the expected outcomes.

I took three of the business-critical objectives, which meant that the business could see that I was committed to the plan, its success and that I was just as prepared for the hard work as I expected them to be. This also meant that at our review meetings, I was accountable to report back to the team on my areas, answer their questions and follow the agreed review protocols. Just as importantly, for the areas that were led by others, I was available, if required, to attend meetings and offer a helping hand or guidance throughout the whole process.

The largest project we undertook, which crossed over all the strategic initiatives and many of the objectives, was the new operating system. So much of the feedback we had received when going through the engagement process could be linked to failings in systems and processes and this was from all the stakeholders. The business operated through spreadsheets, notepads and a reliance on our staff being able to manage manual tasks while generating millions of dollars in revenue and expenditure.

What I knew about software and systems could be written on the back of a stamp, but I wanted to take ownership of this project. It literally cut across every job role and task within the business and that was reason enough for me to take the lead.

It was hard work and 'Murphy's Law' was ever-present. The project involved over one hundred staff members, multiple suppliers, hours of meetings, multiple changes, data creation, data migration, testing and re-testing, but to this day, it was one of the most rewarding projects I have been a part of. I got to work alongside and in every department within the business and uncovered some amazing talent as a consequence.

It also allowed me to learn in detail how each department and most job functions operated, which was invaluable knowledge to have. Above all else, it showed the business that my actions backed my words, and this helped create enthusiasm, a common purpose and kept all the staff engaged through the entire implementation.

I believe managing emotions is an important leadership trait, especially when taking a business through strategic planning. Passion, enthusiasm and excitement are the positive emotions you want to bring to your role, while avoiding negative emotions such as anger, resentment and fear.

The business will be a reflection of you and will feed off your energy and your emotions. It is ok to be angry or frustrated, but you need to be the cool head in the room. Nothing good will come from you yelling or venting to or at your team, and in fact, it can be very damaging to your progress and to the team members in general. If you do need to take someone to task, do it privately and wait a few minutes, as the anger will fade, and you will be in a better frame of mind to have the discussion and to create a positive outcome.

The business and your success are dependent on the success of your people in their roles, and being emotionally intelligent and aware is a key trait of leaders in ensuring their growth and that of the business.

It is the positive emotions that you want the business to see. Passion, enthusiasm, and excitement are infectious – people will gravitate to these emotions, and you will get the best out of a business that lives in this environment.

Maybe it's my sales and marketing background, which is where I started my journey, or maybe it's just common sense, but I think one of the greatest skills a leader can have is to be able to ask questions, and listen to the responses. Asking questions allows you to gain knowledge, understand the problem or issue at hand, and gives you time to think about how you want to reply or what your decision may be.

The question may be as simple as, 'What do you think we should do?' and I always stressed to my team that if they came to me with a problem, they should also provide at least one solution. That enabled me to see how they thought and how they problem-solved.

It also allowed me the opportunity to understand the problem, listen to their solution, and to assess whether their solution was the right one moving forward. I always felt that doing this also provided the opportunity to build a much better rapport between myself and the staff member and it provided a forum to mentor.

Great leaders never stop learning. Whether you've overseen a company for a week, a year, or a lifetime, you are constantly learning. Learning about the next opportunity, learning about new staff members, learning about new customers, and learning about better ways to do things, just to name a few. Leaders should always look to improve their knowledge.

Knowing your business will help with your own leadership skills. When I first took on the role, I knew very little about how the business operated day-to-day. So, I made it my business to spend time in every department to understand what they did, how they did it, why they did it. I didn't need to be the expert, but I needed to have a working knowledge of how everything was completed, why it was done the way it was done, and what the expected outcomes would be.

It is also very important that a leader be decisive. Procrastination and hesitation are the enemies of progress. Gather the facts, seek counsel, and make a decision. If the business is at the crossroads on a particular decision, or a way forward, the leader must make that decision, and the leader must back their decision, and then empower their team to follow that decision through. It may not always work out as hoped, but your ability to be decisive will ensure that in the long run, those decisions are more successful than not.

Following on from being decisive, is being courageous. Just taking the business on this journey is courageous as you are bringing change and there will be times through the implementation of the plan when problems will arise, doubts will seep in, and it may all seem too hard. This is when you need to show your courage and stay the course. Remember, the plan was created off sound principles and the potential outcomes will outweigh the doubt. Yes, it can be tough, but everything worth achieving is, and your courage, or lack of it, will impact the end result.

I will always be grateful for the courage and decisiveness of the president of our company as he didn't hesitate to support our plan in a time of uncertainty, and decreasing markets.

He risked his position to invest in our vision, but then again, I shouldn't be surprised as that's what great leaders do!

There can be a temptation to take on too much or to want to oversee every aspect of the plan. If it is your business or, like me, you are going to be directly held accountable for the outcomes, you can fall into this trap, and it is a trap. Being the business lead does not mean that you are the expert in each area of the business and your team will be better skilled to handle specific areas of the plan. In addition, they have the guidelines by which to operate, and you will be kept updated via the review meetings. If they need your help, they will ask. Your business will be more productive through empowerment than through control and from inception to completion the plan has been built on collaboration and inclusion.

The whole business, no matter how big or small, will be looking to you for leadership and guidance through the implementation of the strategic business plan. This is where the principles or traits of great leadership come to the fore and you should feel confident in the outcomes if you adopt these traits.

Reimagine Leadership:

- Your leadership matters
- Confidence, not ego
- We rather than I
- Lead through inclusion
- Influence over authority
- Actions over words
- The business is a reflection of you
- Managing emotions
- Never stop learning
- Be decisive
- Be courageous

Chapter 8

Recreate the Team

Throughout the book I have spoken about your team and their importance, both in the success of your business in general and when taking the business through strategic planning.

Great leaders, more often than not, have a great team around them and one of the most important roles you have as the leader, if not the most important role, is to build that team. I would always advocate that you actually want to build a team that can replace you. This notion can be very challenging for some people as they fear losing their job or not getting the credit they feel they deserve. Your ego will not create success but might actually ensure failure. I would counter that and propose that by building a great team, and great leaders within that team, you enhance your position and your reputation, which will open doors and opportunities internally and externally for you.

Just as important is to encourage those leaders to build their teams in the exact same way. You want a business that remains agile, you want a business full of leaders, you want people ready for promotion, because the opportunities will come. Your position is to ensure that people are ready to take those opportunities, while knowing they have your support and the support of their peers as they move forward.

Maybe it goes without saying, but I'll say it anyway – you need to trust your team, you need to have empowered them to the point where you trust their decision-making and in turn, they trust you and the guidance and direction you provide. Empowerment begins with trusting someone to complete their role without much oversight and certainly without micromanaging them. You are there for them and yes, you will provide guidance and at times ask for feedback on their progress, but allowing them to develop in the role and develop their skills is the essence of empowerment.

Nothing empowers a person more than trust, constructive guidance, showing appreciation and recognition of achievement and I believe these are the four keys to building better leaders. My last 'golden rule' on empowerment is to not undermine your team. If they make a decision, back that decision, especially in a situation where you have been approached to have it reversed by someone who has gone over their head. If you believe they have made an error, you can give counsel on a way forward, but ultimately and especially for their position, they need to know that you support them.

You are the mentor, and your team will look to you for advice, for guidance and to be decisive, even if the decision is not the one they wanted. Taking time to mentor your team will help in building morale, skills, and better leaders. I was always focused on passing on as much knowledge as I could, whether that be on how they manage within their teams, how they conduct themselves daily, or how they can best succeed moving forward. I saw my job as creating more leaders for the future. By being my direct reports, they were already senior managers, but I wanted them all to have the potential to be in my seat. So, I would spend many hours in one-on-one situations, discussing their concerns, discussing their highlights, and offering my advice as to how they could tackle tricky situations and how they could better improve their skills and their ability.

Your immediate team (direct reports) will heavily influence the success of creating the strategic business plan and especially the successful implementation of that plan. Your team will usually communicate directly with a broader audience than you and as such, you will need them to be as passionate and as committed to the plan as you are.

They have been a critical and significant part of building the plan and through that process they should have been encouraged to challenge the thinking and each aspect of the plan. It is their plan as much as yours and by the time it has been finalised, they should own it and be aligned on the directions the business will take. This level of engagement will ensure their communication, enthusiasm, and passion matches yours.

The key to building a winning team is to have the right people in the right roles. While this applies throughout the business, it is even more vital for your immediate team and the right people are not always the obvious choice. I remember back in the '80s when I was a salesperson, the best salesperson was often made the next sales manager. The best salesperson, however, does not always make the best sales manager. It's a very different role with very different skills, and it's the right skills that you are looking for when building a team around you and those skills are not always the traditional skills for a specific role.

Nearly 20 years ago I met a young lady who was a safety equipment salesperson. I had been asked to review and restructure a branch that was performing badly, and it was so important that I had relocated to that state temporarily to get the job done. I met her at a social engagement and just in talking with her there was that something that you can't quite put your finger on it, but it's there. Never being one to shy away from stepping outside the accepted norm, I offered her a job, but not just any job. I wanted her to be the service manager for that state. She had no experience in the industry, no management experience and no experience managing a team of technicians, parts personnel, and an administration team. If that challenge wasn't going to be daunting enough for her, the fact that it was a male-dominated industry and the company I worked for had no females in operational management roles added another layer of challenges.

However, she bravely took the role, and I took her under my wing and taught her the basics. To cut a long story short, she turned that business around and made that state service department the best in the country. She achieved it because she had amazing people skills, had the instinct to see through the BS, was as tough as nails, and was decisive. She backed her judgement, and she got the job done.

So, when I took on my first company leadership role, I brought her across with me. But again, I threw her another challenge – this time I put her in charge of human resources. We had over 300 staff spread across two countries and nine locations, covering administration, finance, sales, aftermarket service and parts and even manufacturing.

As with the previous role, she used her natural talent, her common-sense approach, and the operational skills she had developed previously to make the HR department a vital part of the operations of the business. Her experience in an operations role provided an extra layer of expertise that might not have occurred otherwise.

Today she remains a senior executive within that organisation and is regarded within the global organisation as the best in practice in her field. In both these roles, she had no formal training when initially taking on the jobs, but she had skills that exceeded anything she would have learned in a classroom. My advice is, trust your instincts, trust your gut. If you think someone is right for a role, and you're prepared to support them in that role, then be brave and make that decision. I know from my perspective; I not only never regretted those decisions, but I learned as much from her as she did from me, and she became one of my most trusted advisors.

While sticking to the theme of talent and women in male-dominated industries, I had two amazing executive assistants during my time in this role who became more than assistants – they became integral members of my team. They brought different skills to the role while in it, but both had skills beyond the role they were in, and their opinion mattered. To prove the point, the first went on to run her own small business, while the second became a senior director in another corporation. This demonstrated another important aspect of a winning team – that just because a person is in a specific role, it does not mean that they are limited to that role or skill set.

I would hope the concept of male-dominated industries or companies is where it should be – gone forever. It should always be the best person for the job, no matter their gender, race, background or their current role.

This leads me into experience versus education. Quite often experience and street smarts will outweigh education, depending on the role. Many of the senior managers that I put in the team prior to creating and rolling out our plan weren't tertiary qualified, but they were very good at what they did, and their experience, passion and knowledge learned was what the business and I needed and is what made them successful.

That doesn't mean that education isn't important and in certain roles, it is clearly essential. However, I am a firm believer that an MBA doesn't necessarily make you a better candidate for a leadership role such as a sales director. Once in the role, training can be provided to ensure any skill gaps are addressed. My point is, if I felt I had the right person for the role, I would take the chance on them, knowing skill gaps can be filled. Trust your instincts.

The size of your team will also impact your ability to be successful. When I first took over the business in 2007, I had more direct reports than I could fit in the meeting room. I knew straight away that was never going to work. So, I started to look at the structure. The reality is I didn't want more than six, or maybe seven direct reports. That's the team that I'm referring to, that core group that you will turn to, to drive the business forward to help build the plan and to execute the plan and its outcomes. Look at your structure prior to commencing the planning for your business future. If you have more than half a dozen direct reports, you probably need to restructure slightly to enable the team to be most effective and to enable you to be the effective leader you need to be.

If you're working in a small business, you might not have a team around you of direct reports. However, you may have contractors that you use to complete certain tasks. These contractors are a major part of your team, especially if you are going through strategic planning. For example, if you outsource your IT, your marketing or any other portion of your business, those contractors should be invited to take part in your business planning. They, potentially, will be part of the implementation of the actions and objectives that the plan has created and, as such, are pivotal to the plan's outcomes. Consider also that having them as part of the process will give them a much better understanding of where you are taking the business and they will be able to offer you better support and service than they would if they were not part of the process.

A major part of empowering your team and making them as effective as possible is to set the ground rules by which you will operate as a team. The ground rules should be simple and easy to follow, while also ensuring structure, support and communication is built in. You also want the ground rules to be transferrable through the whole business. Our ground rules included a weekly staff meeting with a set agenda, our internal communication process, issue resolution process, and expected standards of how we interacted with each other and how the team would interact with their teams.

This is an important step, especially when you are rolling out a significant business plan that is going to change aspects of your business. They don't have to be written down rules, but there must be a clear understanding on how people will work together and how they will work with their teams. This is all part of building culture and, once adopted, disputes were few and far between and when they did happen, they were handled in a professional and courteous manner. I had to ensure that communication was clear, especially following on from our meetings, so our meetings were always minuted, any action points were allocated, and those actions would be how we commenced our next meeting. If something hadn't been completed or had been forgotten, an explanation was sought, and it was re-added for the following week. However, if that continued to be missed, then the necessary actions were taken to understand why and make sure it was rectified for the future.

I feel that it is critical as a leader to be very clear with communication. You don't want to be sending mixed messages or leaving things up to interpretation and I wanted to set the example of what I expected from my team with their communication. Your role encompasses setting the standard and the culture that will transfer through the whole business, so be clear with your communication and expect the same from your team. I also encouraged my team to make sure that their communication was frequent with their teams and so on through the business.

Team building is often overlooked or, when done, lacks purpose. When we did our strategic planning meetings, there would always be a half-day for a team-building exercise. On one occasion, in an Olympic year, we had our own version of the Olympics, where we put on some fun sports, from table tennis to pinball to beach cricket. We actually allocated gold, silver and bronze medals specially made for the events. On another occasion we went paintballing, which is not uncommon, but we had two former SAS soldiers speak to the team and share their experiences. When it came time to splatter each other in paint, it was done with a purpose created around working together as a team.

These events, while fun, had a deeper purpose and that was to see how the team interacted, to understand the different personality types and for me to then evaluate how they could best work together for their and the business' benefit. Not everyone is outgoing, we are all motivated in different ways and team-building is an opportunity to see the team dynamic. It helped me develop my management style to suit each individual while ensuring the best team dynamic.

Recognise and reward your team publicly, as this is not only the right thing to do but will only further enhance their want to succeed as part of your team. One of my duties was to always build my team up and never criticise them in public. As discussed in the chapter on leadership, if the business achieved its goals, it was that we achieved our goals, and I would single out my team members and praise them to America to ensure that they were recognised for their hard work, that they felt valued as part of being in my team. This built a stronger team that craved further success.

If the need arose to be critical of a team member it was done privately, in my office or over the phone and never in front of their peers or their teams. I was always more critical of poor behaviour rather than mistakes. Mistakes will happen, but poor behaviour such as belittling a teammate, being offensive or just rude should never be tolerated. Apart from the personal harm it can cause, it will splinter a team and create division that may never be repaired.

If it is a mistake, you have had the 'tough conversation' and it's now resolved, you should ensure they understand that you continue to have their back and you continue to want them to succeed. Their peers don't need to know anything else about the situation other than it has been resolved and ended up being a positive experience.

Finally, you will always have, or should at least want, diversity within your team and this is a positive as you don't want clones. If your team doesn't challenge you, then maybe, it's not the right team or you are not the right leader.

Recreate the Team:

- Be replaceable
- Right people, right roles
- Experience versus education
- Establish the ground rules
- Empower your team
- Clear and consistent communication
- Team building
- Reward and recognition
- Mentoring

Chapter 9

Redefine the Basics

There are some basics that while obvious, when we go through them, need to be mentioned, because they are so often overlooked.

I have talked about communication throughout the book and there is a reason I want to mention it again. It is at the heart of every aspect of a successful business and critical to business planning, stakeholder engagement, morale, culture and ensuring a common purpose.

I communicated progress updates to the business in two specific ways: firstly via email, which were sent as key milestones were achieved, and secondly, via face-to-face meetings in our different locations when I travelled. As part of our ongoing engagement process with our staff, we held end-of-month barbeques and I would travel to a different location each month and provide a general business and business plan update to the teams.

My golden rule is, don't fear sharing information with the business. This is not just while going through business planning, but also in general. If you are serious about having the business engaged, then respect them enough to provide real updates. While I didn't go through detailed financial updates, I would give an overview of business performance, good or bad, and the same applied during the business planning and implementation process. At times, we fell behind in rolling out some of the actions, and being honest and open about it will gain more traction than to avoid or misrepresent the situation.

I expected no less from my team. This was the culture we built through the business, and it held us in good stead when it mattered most.

Our customers and suppliers also received email updates, and personal ones when I met with them. In addition, we created two magazines, one for general reading and the second specific to the aftermarket business. Both magazines were sent out as printed hard copies as well as email soft copies. These magazines commenced as an action within the plan for our customers and were so popular that we often had to do a second print to meet demand. We featured a different customer business in each edition and provided them artwork for their own marketing activities.

Some of our key suppliers even advertised within the magazines as our customer base was also theirs. This meant the magazines were cost-neutral, but more importantly, were a wanted and valued communication tool.

Communication, which was one of our perceived weaknesses, became one of our key strengths and assisted in building a strong customer bond.

The rarest commodity in business and in general appears to be common sense and if you doubt me on this one, I would like you to think about the 'Darwin Awards' which are given out each year in recognition of all the stupid ways people have found to accidentally kill themselves. Sad but true, and worth a Google.

ISO (International Organisation for Standardisation) was established to help businesses by creating standards by which they operate aimed at meeting customer and stakeholder needs. The standards they create are invaluable to businesses globally, but interestingly some, such as ISO9002 – the ISO created guidelines for quality assurance in installation, production, and service provision – are basic common sense and were created because common sense didn't exist or at the very least, wasn't being applied. Companies around the world have spent millions of dollars to become ISO certified or, when it comes to safety, try to be idiot proof.

When it comes to business planning or leading a business, common sense will be your greatest asset, but it starts with you, not a standard. It starts with temperament and staying calm in a crisis. It's hard for anyone to make rational decisions if the first response is to panic. Take a moment to understand the situation and always aim for a root cause solution.

For example, as we began to be more customer-focused, our aftermarket team prioritised a quick response to a customer machine breakdown. This was a great start, however the problem kept reoccurring and on several machines. On each occasion they prioritised the repair, but eventually, as the problems kept occurring the customers stopped caring about how quickly we fixed it and became frustrated with what they saw as an inherent problem with the equipment, so it hit my desk. I asked some basic questions, and one was 'I understand you keep swapping out the part to fix the issue, but what is the cause of the failure?' In their haste to get the machine working, no one had examined what was causing the failure. The machines impacted were examined and in simple terms it was the wrong part being fitted, so while it would work for a while, it would eventually fail. The correct part was fitted, and the problems stopped. It's ok to fix the problem but understanding what caused the problem will provide the root cause solution.

My point is, if something keeps going wrong then there is usually a root cause that has not yet been identified and finding this is the common sense approach.

You set the standard for common sense. My tips are to stay calm, ask questions, find the root cause and be flexible. The plan might have a particular action or objective that, as it is worked on, proves to be inadequate or irrelevant and as such persisting is pointless. Use your common sense tools and either seek an alternative or drop it altogether.

One of the certainties as you implement your plan is that something will go wrong. It is not a matter of if, but when. That is ok – your planning has anticipated changes and as long as your process has been sound, you will have a risk and mitigation and if you don't for the particular problem, you just create one.

The planning and implementation process will also create additional opportunities not identified initially, or enhance an existing opportunity, and these should not be ignored. Your review process will allow you to explore the additional opportunity and its value, to write it into the plan and allocate the resources to make it happen.

Our plan included documenting processes and procedures and this was enhanced when the software partner introduced us to a lady who specialised in linking our tasks with how they were actioned in the new system. We then created a new objective and actions that meant, through this lady, we created work instructions and procedures for every task in the business. The result was a detailed 'how-to' manual for the business. It became an invaluable training tool and meant that anyone in the business could do any task by following the appropriate document. It gave us an added benefit of being able to use temporary staff, should the need arise, and have them productive from the moment they sat down.

There are many little things you can do to make the planning and implementation successful. One of the first steps in creating the plan was to create the vision for the future, something which can be overlooked or forgotten as you work through the implementation. With this in mind we had it published, along with the business values, and had them framed and hung in each reception and each manager's office. It may seem a minor consideration, but it kept our long-term goals front of mind and you would be surprised how often visitors commented or wanted to discuss them.

If your engagement and ongoing communication with your customers is building stronger relationships, then you can also seek their support on some of your objectives, should that be appropriate. Our largest customer was looking to implement the same software and operating system as us and this became an opportunity to work together to improve the way our business connected. Together we developed a B2B system that allowed them to order parts, machines, and services directly through our software and this was in a time before this type of connection was standard as it is today.

The plan you have created has been built on verified data, and the strategic initiatives, objectives and actions within the plan are therefore not just a roadmap to where you want to be, but also principles by which you want to operate as a business.

Use those principles in the day-to-day decision-making, even before the plan has been implemented. If your plan has a strategic initiative to 'improve the customer experience', then instil this in the business prior to implementing the plan and have this concept at the front of mind when they are dealing with a customer. In other words, this is the culture embedded in the plan and you want to create and deliver the culture faster, as this will enhance the desired outcomes within the plan.

The marketing plan should be created as part of the strategic business plan and not a separate document. I detailed earlier how the finance team created our budget and forecasts as we created our objectives and actions. This gave us an immediate sanity check on whether what we were proposing was going to stack up and meant we had a working financial plan linked to the business plan from day one. The same principles apply to marketing. You want the marketing activities created as actions to support the objectives within your plan and you will need the marketing team to understand what it is the business is trying to achieve.

The final basic I want to raise is belief. If you don't believe in what you are undertaking, you can't expect the business or your market to. From belief comes commitment and you need to be committed for this or any aspect of what you undertake for the business to succeed. If you start the strategic business planning process, then see it through. I have seen a business that went through planning and created a great plan that was clearly going to get them from where they were to where they wanted to be, but they decided not to implement it as they felt 'there were other priorities that were more important'. The impact was felt over time as their staff became disillusioned, their customers remained frustrated, and the business suffered through poor financial performance. Eight months later, they wanted to fast track implementation as they realised their position, but by then, the plan needed to be reviewed and the process started from scratch. The challenge was regaining the trust lost with their stakeholders. They eventually revised the plan and implemented it, but by their own admission, they hurt their position and it took a long time to regain the lost ground. Believe in what the planning can do and be committed to it. I was open with the business leader and once the dust had settled, I reminded him that the business is a reflection of you in every way and this concept should be your guide in how you do your job and how you drive your business. He smiled and said, 'Yep, I won't make that mistake again'.

One of the great benefits of business planning is how it can help you focus on the basics. Those basics can enhance the outcomes for your business well beyond what was projected in the plan. Whether it be improved communication, customer and staff relationships or additional opportunities, planning will help you with the fundamentals of your business that may have been lost or overlooked through the pressure of daily operations.

Redefine the Basics:

- Enhanced communication
- Sharing information
- Common sense
- Additional opportunities
- Change as needed
- Instil the plan principles in the day-to-day focus
- Improved focus on the basics
- Belief and commitment

Chapter 10

Recreate the Outcomes

It doesn't matter whether your business is already successful, is struggling or is a new venture, taking it through strategic business planning is all about achieving the outcomes. There are some outcomes that might not necessarily be in the plan itself – one of these is to see the positive changes that occur within the business by undergoing business planning.

On each occasion I took a business through strategic business planning there was a marked increase in staff satisfaction, engagement and morale. Giving your staff a voice and for them to know they have been listened to is the catalyst for this and don't underestimate the improvement in productivity that follows. The flow on then impacts your customers as they begin to deal with a motivated workforce and, when you need your staff to take on additional duties associated with implementing the plan, you will get little resistance. In fact, in my experience, you will have people volunteering, as they see the benefits for themselves in the plan and what it will bring.

Even if you have strong customer relationships prior to planning, it is likely that there will still be some objectives and actions that focus on maintaining and improving that relationship. In our case, we had a disillusioned customer base and therefore many objectives and actions aimed at improving the customer relationship. If you have completed the customer engagement, then your customers will notice the change and just as importantly, the intent. This inevitably creates opportunities for additional business with those customers.

One of the objectives that we had established was to 'increase customer spend by 10%' and this was under the strategic initiative of 'improve the customer experience'. This may seem odd at first glance, however, the actions assigned to that objective were all focused on fixing the issues that existed for our customers. Our premise was that if we addressed the issues that our customers had outlined, that we could then chase the additional sales and the growth would follow. I remember that it was questioned by America at the time, not just for the approach, but also because we were committing to millions of dollars of additional business that we would be held accountable for.

We changed our marketing focus and, instead of the traditional marketing concept of advertising our products, created a campaign focused purely on our customers' needs and our actions to improve their perception of our business. Of course, this would only work if we delivered the required changes and so our timing was important, however as we commenced delivering on our plan and it was being noticed, we were able to capitalise on the improvements and the marketing was seen by the customers as a positive and humble step forward. The result was a 14% increase in existing customer sales in the first year and over 20% in year two.

Of course, we chased new business as well and that was captured in the plan, however my example is to highlight the outcomes that can be achieved through effective customer engagement, using this feedback to build a plan, and then executing the plan to meet their needs. It also highlights that through effective planning, you can change thinking. Our marketing approach changed because our thinking changed, as had the needs of our business. This is another part of being agile and, importantly, being brave enough to challenge tradition or what has 'always been done' before.

As companies grow, there is often a trend where departments become isolated or operate as almost separate entities within the business. This itself can cause problems, with everything from communication to purpose and standards of operating. Business planning breaks this cycle as every area of the business is involved and comes together with a common purpose and an agreed direction.

It won't happen just because you are in planning mode, however any friction between areas is usually obvious and this creates the opportunity to break down the cause and bring the teams together during the planning sessions.

One of my favourite outcomes from strategic business planning is finding the hidden talent within the business. Without exception, every time I have taken a business through planning someone has stepped up and shown leadership skills or skills above their current position. It provides you with a wonderful opportunity to nurture that talent for the future and create succession planning that will strengthen the business for years to come.

Strategic business planning provides outcomes such as 'best practice principles' to become your standard operating procedure. The outcomes encompass creating engagement as part of your business process, ongoing communication, planning for change, creating a path forward and being agile when circumstances change. At the same time, you have a structured business performance review process which allows for streamlining how you operate, remaining customer and staff-focused, and delivering outstanding results.

Businesses that regularly plan for the future tend to have high customer and staff satisfaction and retention, are more focused and better organised generally.

Our results exceeded even what we had expected and were highlighted by record revenue and market share levels for the next four years, record profit levels for the same period, the R.O.I on capex completed in nine months, lowest staff turnover levels ever recorded, the beginning of several 'Supplier of the Year' awards, and best practice process, just to mention a few. Most importantly to me, though, was having a business that people outside the company wanted to work for, and having a senior executive team that continued to lead the business for nearly a decade after I had left.

We continued to go through the planning process each year, even if we were mid-plan, to ensure we were listening to our customers, staff and suppliers and to give the existing plan a health check. There was always something we could add, change or modify, but of most importance to me was that it kept the business agile, focused and ready for whatever was to come next.

I was at an industry function a couple of years after the plan had been implemented and the leader of one of our competitors said to me, 'You sure did get lucky'. I just smiled rather than saying anything, but I was thinking about the Roman philosopher, Seneca, who said 'Luck is when preparation meets opportunity'.

Yes, we capitalised on the mining boom, but we also survived the global financial crisis better than our competition because we took a business that, on paper, was doing well, but was really fragile and we planned our way forward. We created a new level of engagement, we planned the path forward and implemented it successfully, we created our own luck, we redefined the business, we reimagined the possibilities and we recreated the future.

Recreate the outcomes:

- Outcomes are not all in the plan
- Outcomes are not always financial
- Step outside traditional concepts
- Bring the business together
- Find hidden talent
- Best practice business principles
- Preparation meets opportunity

About the Author

A ndrew Satterley is an award-winning business leader whose career has predominately been focused through Asia Pacific and the United States.

Andrew grew up in Melbourne with a passion for sport and was known as a fierce competitor with a drive to win, something which transferred to his working life. Starting in sales, he quickly established himself as a top performer and developed his first sales training package, which became the standard for new salespeople in that company. His passion, however, was in understanding the workings of the business and developing ways for it to improve.

When he took on his next role, Andrew made it his business to understand the systems and processes behind the sales and, once given a management opportunity, his real skills came to the fore.

Starting at Crown Equipment, Andrew rose through the ranks, starting as a salesperson before eventually becoming General Manager of Asia Pacific for the rental division. He then moved to Linde Materials Handling as General Manager of Sales and Marketing. Andrew was then appointed as Managing Director for JLG Industries Australia and New Zealand before being promoted to Vice President and Managing Director for

Asia Pacific. Andrew also led NACCO Materials Handling Asia Pacific, Adaptalift Hyster and Baseplan Software. Andrew was 'head-hunted' for all his senior management roles, and was eventually given the opportunity to lead a global blue-chip company within the Asia Pacific region.

Andrew's strengths include uncovering talent, building winning teams, challenging and improving the how and why things are done, focusing on listening to the customers and staff and then developing and implementing business plans that create success and sustainability, no matter the economic climate. It was these attributes that helped to build his reputation as a 'must-have' leader, and he was subsequently sought out by companies wanting that level of success.

When talking with Andrew, his passion, common-sense and business intelligence shine through and further enhance his position as a renowned business leader and someone to be listened to. He firmly believes that even successful businesses can do better and that success is not luck, but rather an approach, an attitude, a series of steps and a common purpose.

'Create an environment where we all work hard, but it's not hard work.'

Andrew Satterley

Contact details:
Email business@andrewsatterley.com.au
Website www.andrewsatterley.com.au

Notes

Notes

Redefine Reimagine Recreate

Notes